PRIVATE LESSONS

Jazz Hanon

By Peter Deneff

ISBN 0-634-01873-6

7777 W. BLUEMOUND RD. P.O. BOX 13819 MILWAUKEE, WI 53213

Copyright © 2001 by HAL LEONARD CORPORATION
International Copyright Secured   All Rights Reserved

Visit Hal Leonard Online at
www.halleonard.com

This book is dedicated to
George V. Deneff

About the author

Peter Deneff is a pianist, composer, producer, and teacher in southern California. He began playing at age three and started his formal training at nine with classical pianist Leaine Gibson. He began jazz studies in 1986 with pianist Mike Garson. He studied composition at California State University Long Beach with Dr. Justus Matthews and Dr. Martin Herman. He is currently furthering his musical studies at CSULB, recording, and performing a spicy blend of Middle Eastern and Latin jazz with his band, Excursion. He also teaches privately and at the Orange County High School of the Arts. He resides in southern California with his wife Diane, and his children, Gitana, George and Sophia.

Introduction

Of all the different genres of music, I would consider jazz to be one of the most technically challenging, both mentally and physically. For instance, one must interpret the harmony of a jazz piece through a series of voicings. Furthermore, the jazz pianist is often expected to simultaneously craft an improvisation. As if this weren't enough of a challenge, they might also be required to give cues to the rest of the band. Blazing tempi, complex melodic lines and intricate harmonic progressions challenge even the most seasoned musicians.

With all of the cerebral resistance one deals with when navigating through a jazz tune, it would seem logical that the pianist should at least prepare their fingers for the task. I have always believed that a good musician should never be limited by their lack of good technique. Technique is not an end in itself but rather a "tool" in the pianist's "toolbox". Classical pianists by the nature of their repertoire seem to be exposed to technical exercises from an early age. Rarely have I come across a serious piano student who has not played through C.L. Hanon's *The Virtuoso Pianist*, Czerny or other books of finger exercises. It would seem impossible to venture through a Bach fugue or a Scriabin etude without proper technical preparation.

While the traditional books of piano technique are paramount in the study of most piano literature, they do not address many of the challenges the jazz pianist faces. Angular lines, large intervallic leaps, pentatonic patterns, irregular chromatic melodies, and unconventional (in a classical sense) fingerings need to be practiced in a formal and organized manner in order to be executed articulately and evenly. These are the things on which I concentrate most in this book. While traditional books of technique should not be discarded, these exercises will provide an invaluable source of challenging practice material for all pianists, but especially for those who play jazz. The beginner as well as the professional will find them useful for building, improving, and maintaining their physical ability.

There are many ways that one could practice the studies in this book. They can be played as written using straight eighths, or with a swing feel. The right hand lines could be played in unison with the left hand "à la Oscar Peterson." Lastly, one could play the right hand part with the left and vise versa.

I did not include tempo markings because I don't believe in limiting how fast these exercises should be practiced. At the same time, however, they should never be played faster than they can be performed cleanly and free of mistakes. The key to playing fast is practicing slowly, and building the tempo incrementally. This is a practice technique that is almost always neglected by overzealous students! Some other techniques I like to use when practicing these exercises include the following:

- Start very slowly, deliberately, and staccato. This helps build articulation.

- Use a metronome. It will help build your sense of time.

- When you master an exercise at a given speed, increase the tempo **one notch** on your metronome.

- Keep your hands low profile and your fingers curved.

- Don't tense up. Monitor the tension in your **entire body**.

- Push yourself, but stop if you are experiencing pain. Technique exercises won't help you if you injure yourself!

The main thing to keep in mind is that you should have fun with these exercises. Be creative and find new ways to incorporate these techniques into your music, jazz or otherwise. Last but not least, don't get discouraged by delayed progress. We all learn and develop at our own rate. Technique doesn't happen overnight. It may take weeks or even months to master some of these exercises, but when you do, you will have gained much of what is needed to become the next great jazz pianist!

Happy playing,
Peter Deneff

1

2

3

4

5

6

8

9

10

25

11

12

14

16

17

18

19

20

22

23

24

51

25

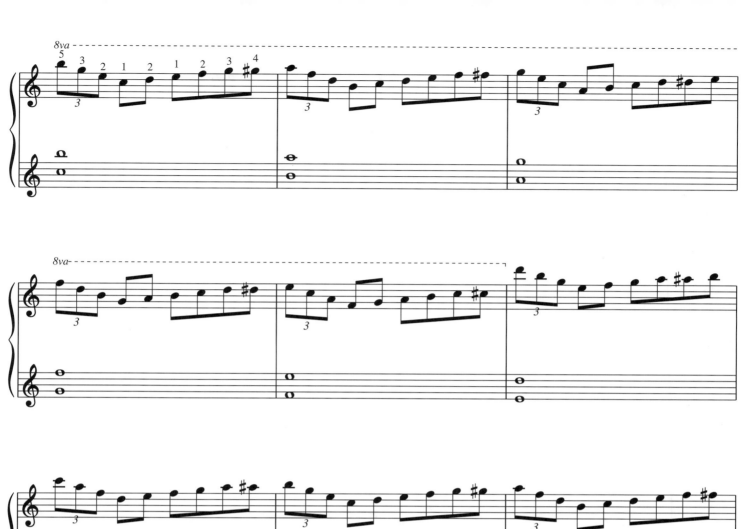

26

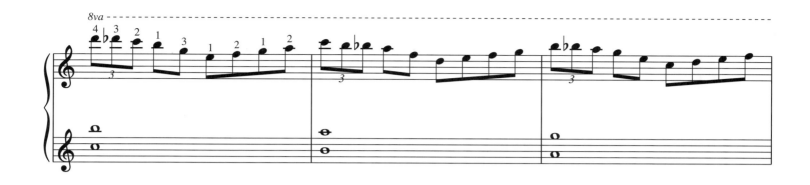

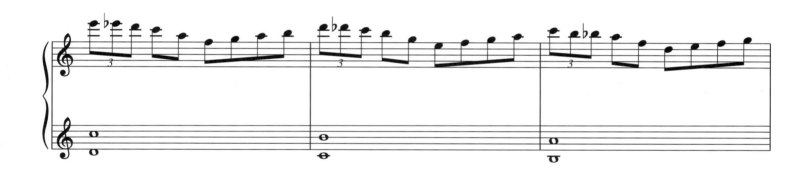

27

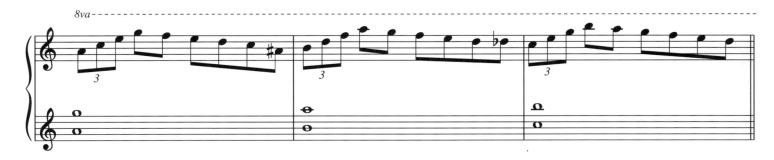

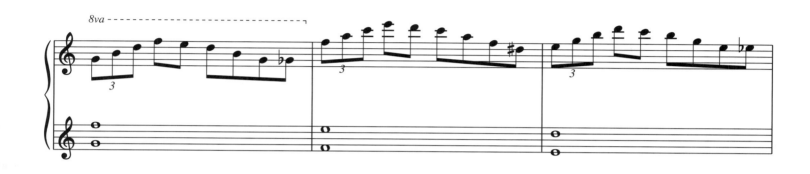

28

29

30

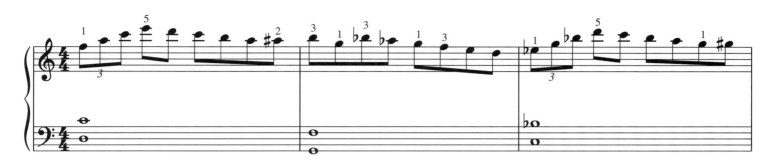

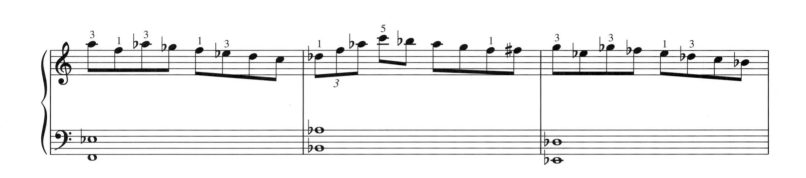

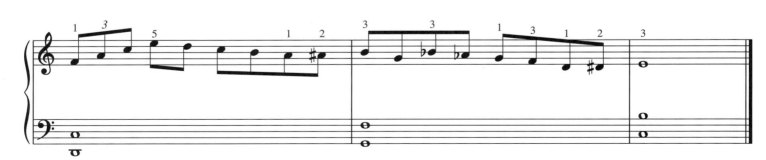

31

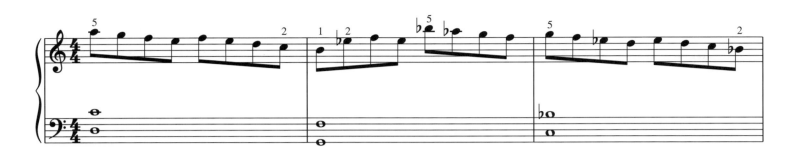

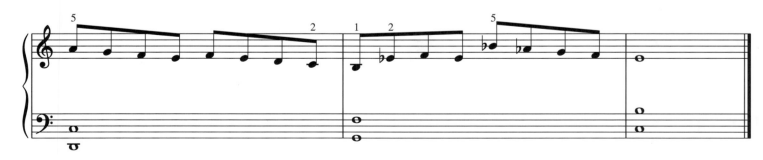

32

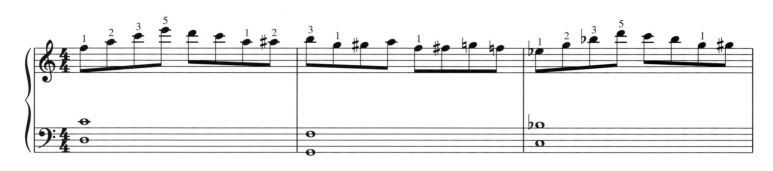

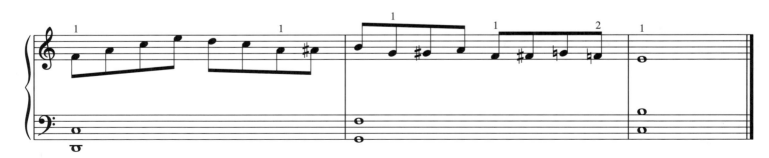

33

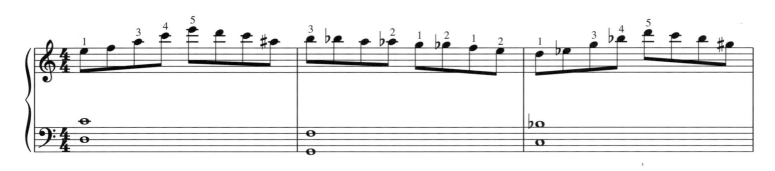

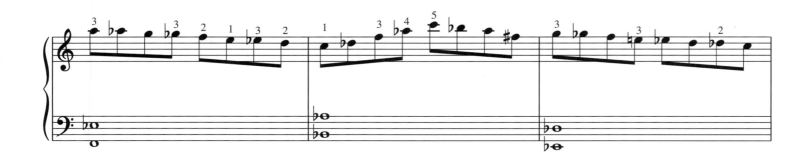

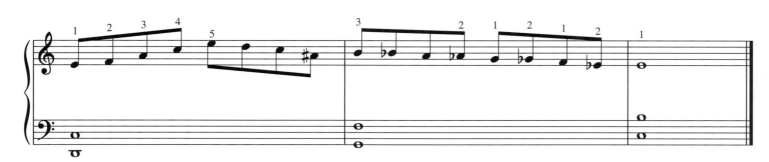

34

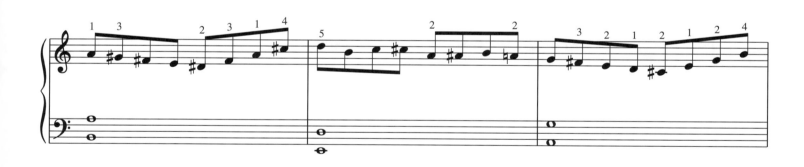

35

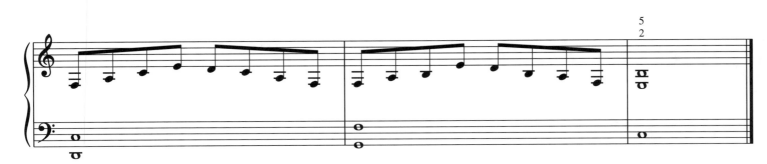

36

37

38

39

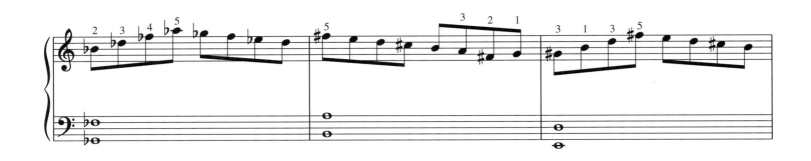

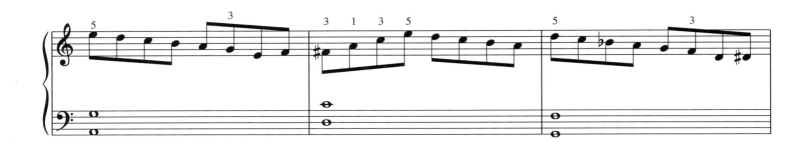

40

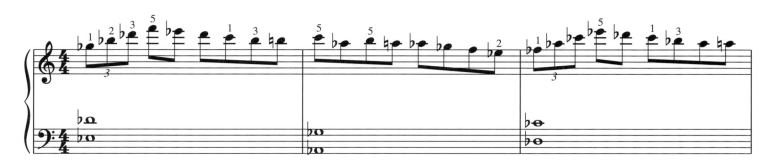

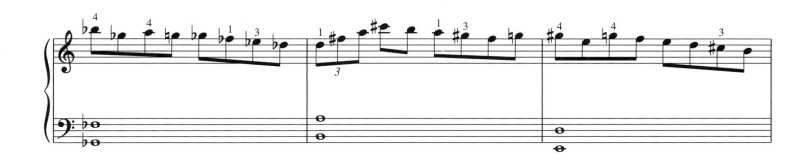

41

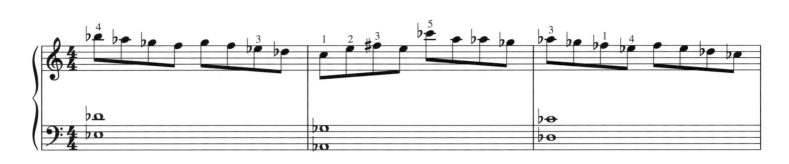

42

43

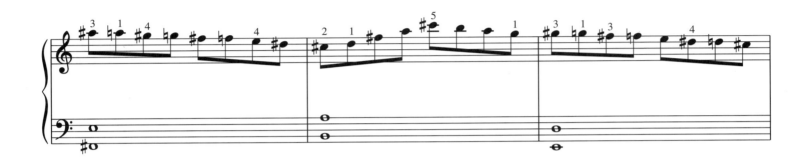

44

45

46

47

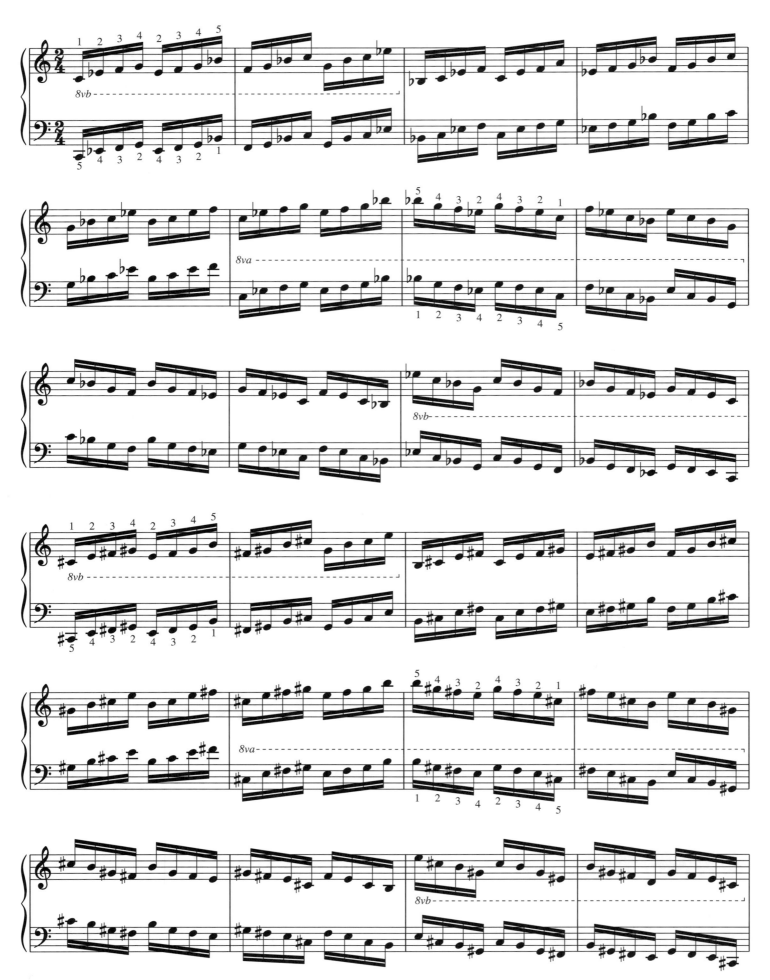

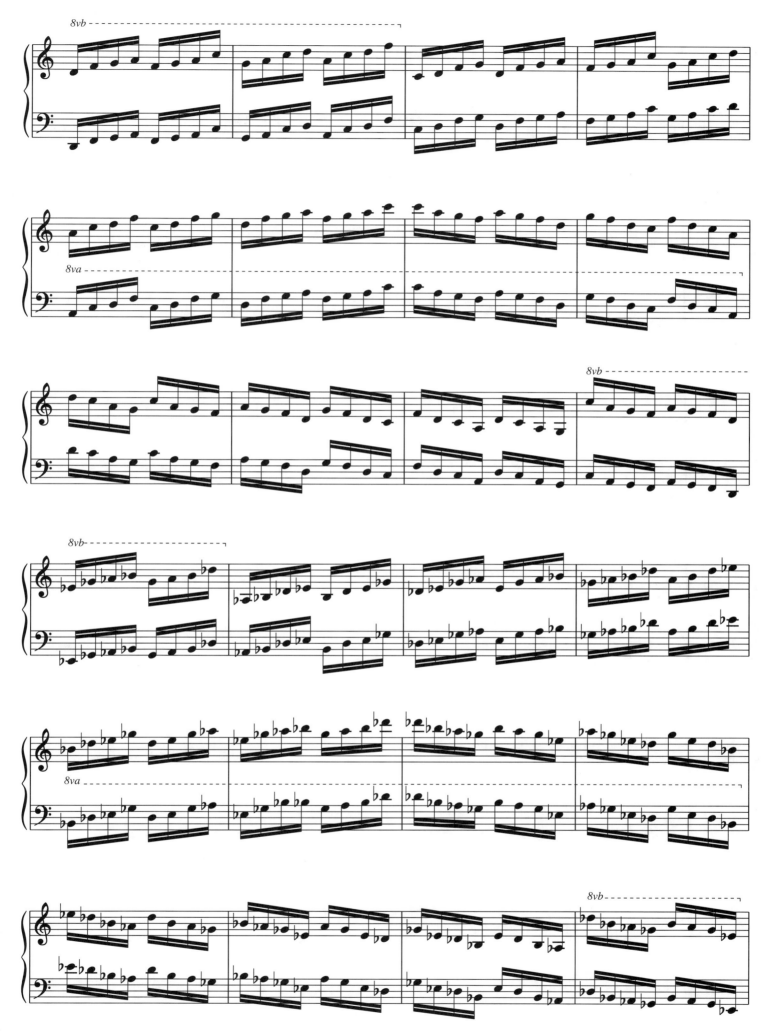

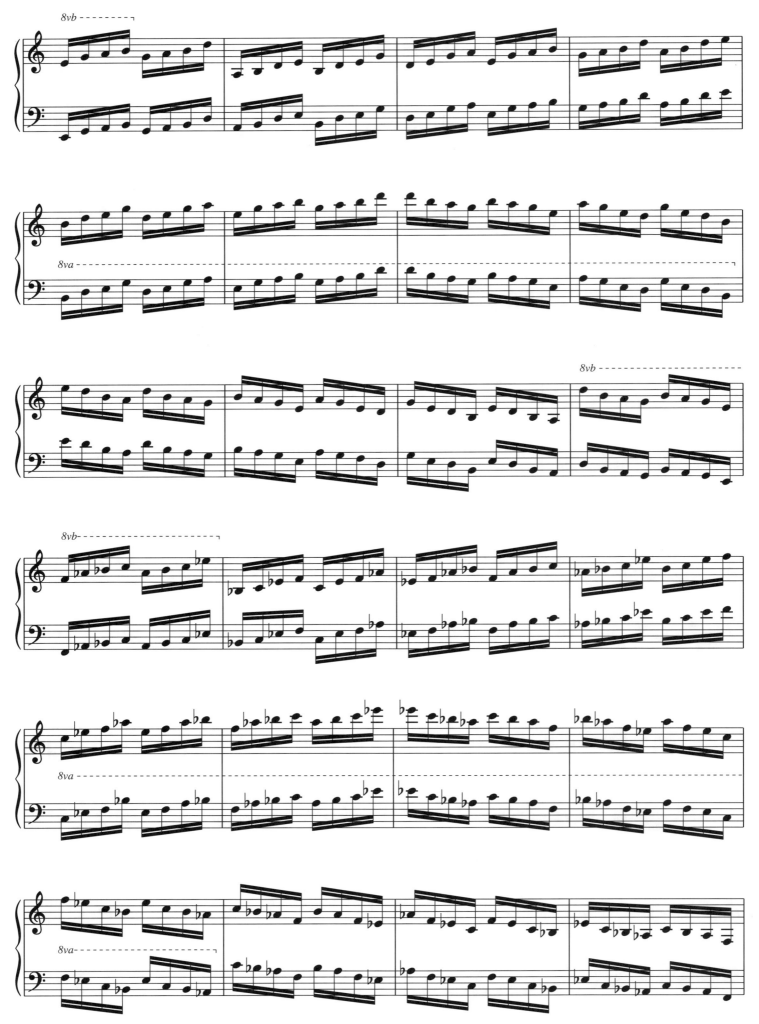

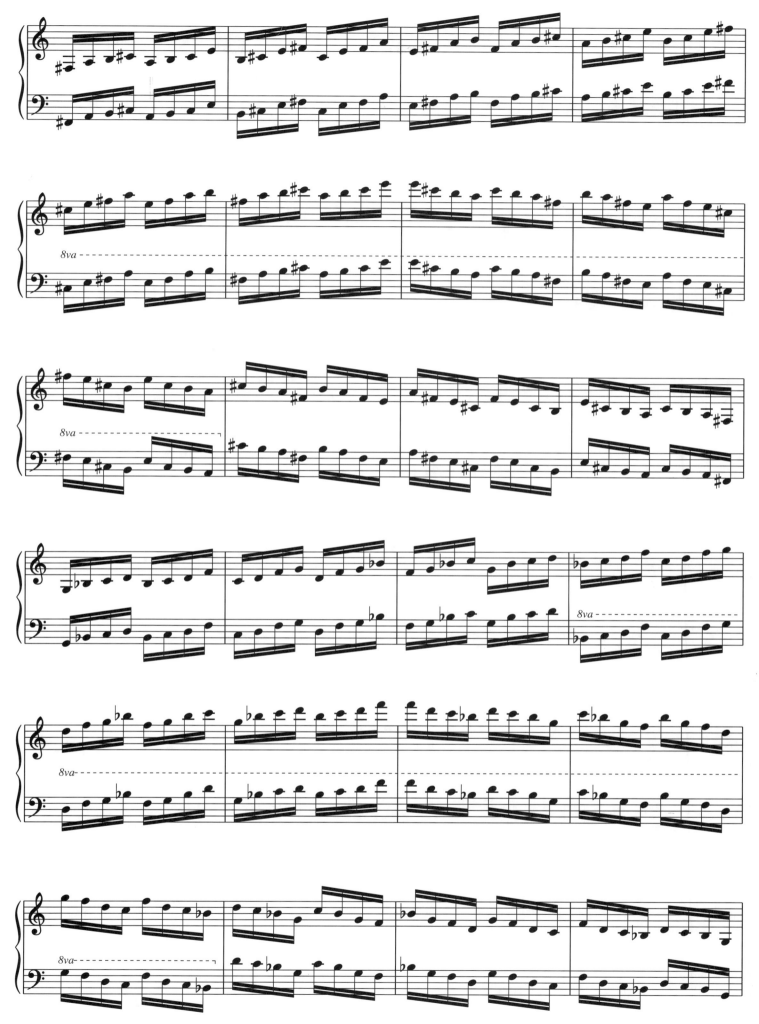

81

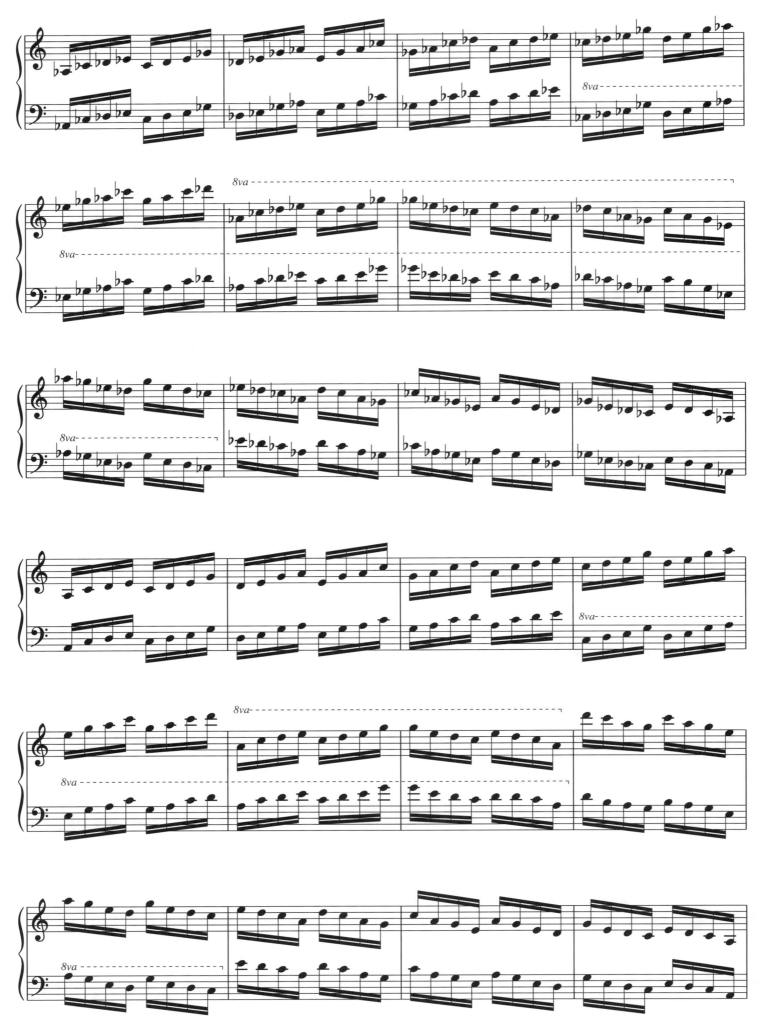

48

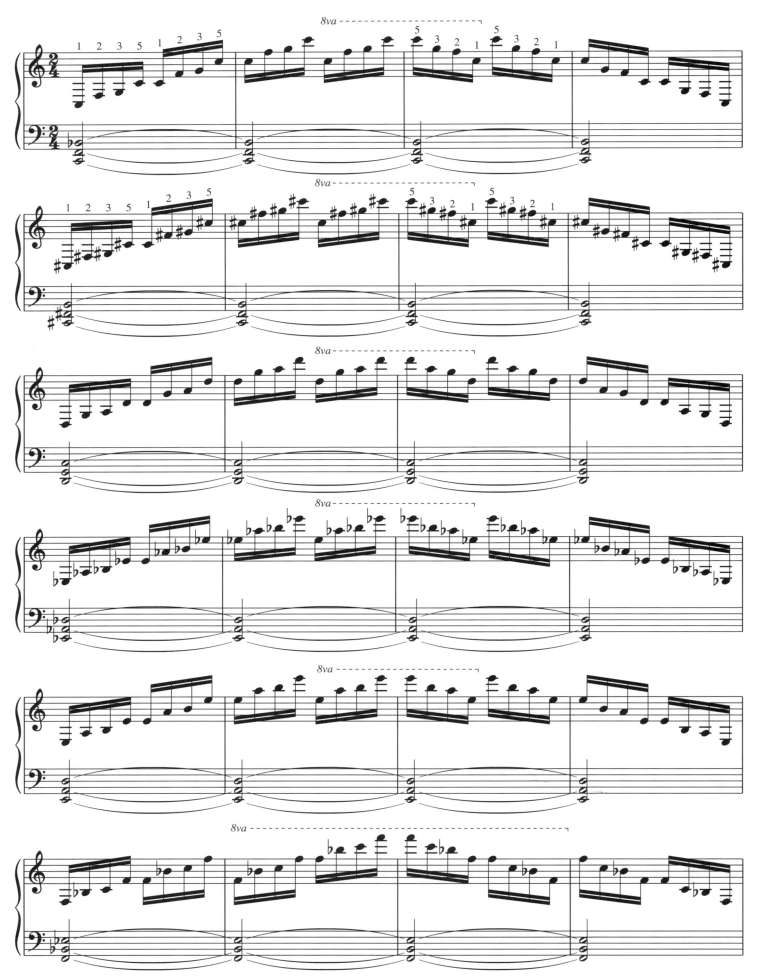

49

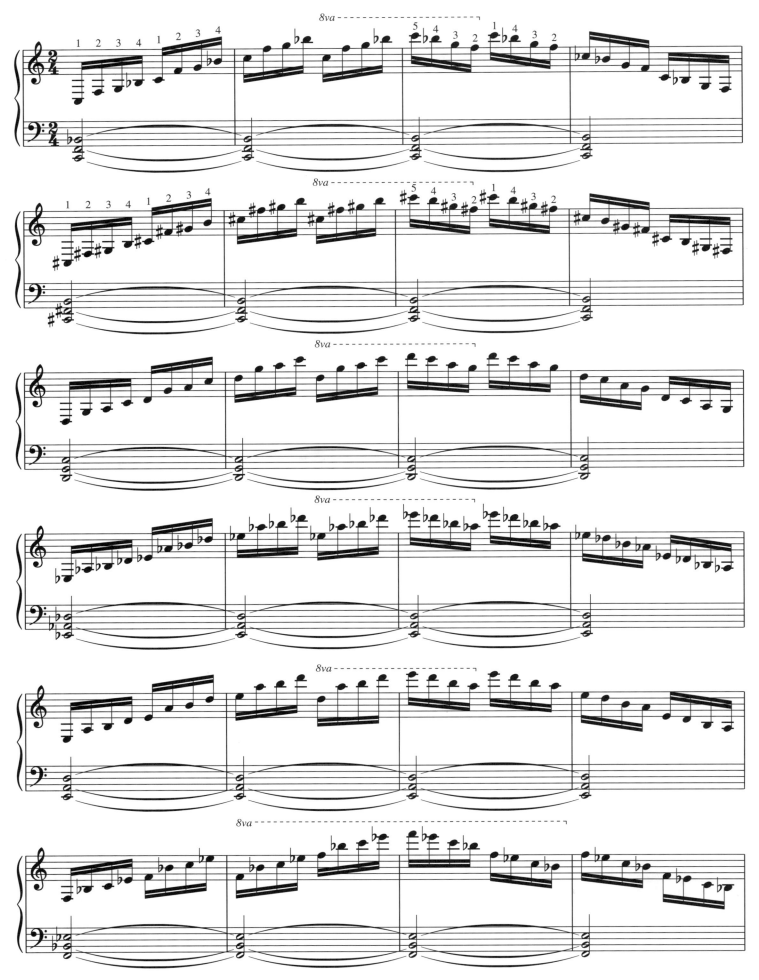

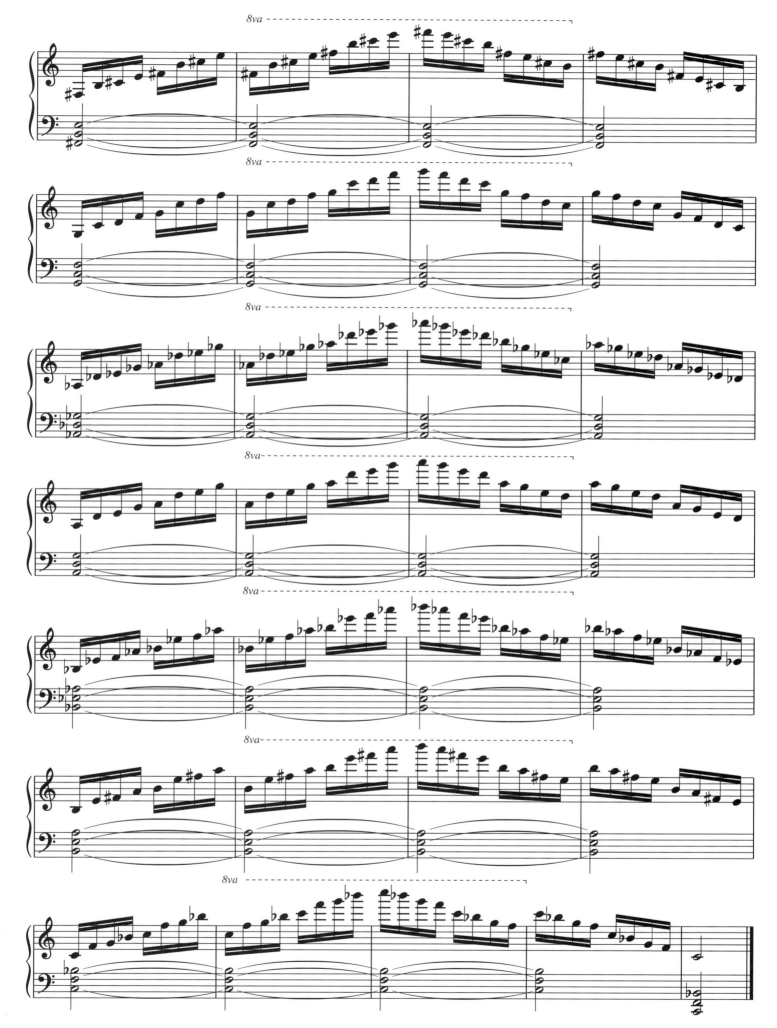

50